Cuentos from the Swamp

poems by

Michelle Lizet Flores

Finishing Line Press
Georgetown, Kentucky

Cuentos from the Swamp

Copyright © 2019 by Michelle Lizet Flores
ISBN 978-1-64662-044-9 First Edition
All rights reserved under International and Pan-American Copyright Conventions.
No part of this book may be reproduced in any manner whatsoever without written permission from the publisher, except in the case of brief quotations embodied in critical articles and reviews.

ACKNOWLEDGMENTS

I'd like to thank the following publications where versions of these poems first appeared:

Palabra: "A Song for JP and Quireña," and "La Pata Caliente"
Badlands: "Ode to a Papi Chulo," "Ode to a Chonga," and "Guajira Trapped in the States"
The Miami Rail: "Florida Gothic #1: The Colony," "Florida Gothic #2: Hogar," "Florida Gothic #3: I-10 to Lake City"
N*oble/Gas Quarterly*: "Giving Up La Lucha"
Gravel Magazine: "Self-Taught Motherhood" and "Of Dora and Diego"
Azahares: "Sugarloaf Key" and "Eliseo"
Rigorous: "Mateo Sings the Blues"
Cagibi: "Hurricane Season"
Clockhouse: "The Flying Flor"

Publisher: Leah Maines
Editor: Christen Kincaid
Cover Art: Kiara Amaris Sanchez
Author Photo: George Varkanis
Cover Design: Elizabeth Maines McCleavy

Printed in the USA on acid-free paper.
Order online: www.finishinglinepress.com
also available on amazon.com

Author inquiries and mail orders:
Finishing Line Press
P. O. Box 1626
Georgetown, Kentucky 40324
U. S. A.

Table of Contents

Hurricane Day 1

The Flying Flor 2

Sugarloaf Key 3

Florida Gothic #2: Hogar 4

La Pata Caliente 6

Ode to a Chonga 7

Eliseo 8

Ode to a Papi Chulo 10

New Year's Eve's Eve 11

Hurricane Season 13

Alone 14

Dressing my Mother 15

Guajira Trapped in the States 16

Giving Up La Lucha 17

Of water 18

A Nighttime Stroll 19

Florida Gothic #1: The Colony 20

A Song for JP and Quireña 21

Mateo Sings the Blues 22

Of Dora and Diego 23

Crabtree Park 24

Self-Taught Motherhood 25

Florida Gothic #3: I-10 to Lake City 26

Hurricane Day

I dive into the cold briny water. October winds roll the waves towards shore. I kick my way to the depths while I stare at the waves above me, the cloudy jade water breaking, forcing me down onto the sand. I pop up for air, and a wave smashes into my face. I laugh and cough, diving back before another can hit me. I look eerie beneath the surface. My skin hasn't seen real sunlight in almost five months. I am ghost, a victim of the siren's call, trying to make my way back to my ship. As I glide back up, I scan the shore. My sister sits with her knees to her chest, arms wrapped around legs, and I slowly swim to her.

When the water is shallow enough, I climb onto the rough sand, plopping myself down beside her. She hides her face in her knees. Her long, black hair covers her back and shoulders. She peeks at me, head still pressed against her knees, eyes dry and dark. I pull some of the thick black curls away from her face.

"I miss her," she says. I glance at the water.

"I miss her too." We sit on the beach while tourists and teenagers shift about, playing soccer and blasting their radios. I wipe my eyes and lie on my back, squinting while staring at the bright sky above. Faint wisps of white float above me, then her hair whips against the sky. I prop myself up as she dives into the ocean. When she comes up for air, her hair floats around her. She turns towards shore, then slips back into the water. I sit up with my legs crossed, pushing my hands into the sand.

The Flying Flor

She floats, suspended around the waist from our rusty swing set by the neon green jump rope I won after selling eight boxes of the world's finest chocolate, her deep brown hair flying around her freckled face, her lips hugging her oversized teeth while she sings her Spanish songs, arms raised, calling on the winds to pick her up and take her away; for a moment they do, but I lose faith and there she falls, the glitter-filled rope snapping, releasing her down to the ground in a daze of terrified giggles and flailing limbs.

As I run to her, she rolls over, face contorted, a fallen seraph punctured by the blades of grass, while Abuela scuttles outside, ammonia and brown dye number 37 dripping down her cheek, melting her brows into hazel eyes, hands still covered by too-big plastic gloves; she picks up The Flying Flor, smacks her, checks to see if she's all right, then comes after me, popping my nalgas before I have time to brace myself.

I limp towards my broken jump rope as she is carried inside, the neon stretched to whiteness, dreams of greatness dashed as I realize hubris is the lie we tell ourselves when we attempt to fly without wings.

Sugarloaf Key

For the first time in a long time,
I can see the stars.
Hell, I can see the Milky Way—
the sky is finally more than a haze of street lamps.
Papi's putting away the fishing poles while
Mom and Nicky play a card game of ten phases.
I can never remember the rules.

I hear the ocean. It drifts in and out.
I want to dive in the dark water.
I want to search for jellyfish and mermaids.
I want to find Atlantis and see what all the fuss is about.

"Chelly," Papi calls. "Ven aquí. Hold me this."
He passes me a plate of steaks for the grill.
Sirens beckon me towards the water, but we have to eat.
Our tent shakes in a gust of wind.

"Dame el plato." He takes the plate from my hands
and I set the table. The sirens give up, moving further
south, perhaps to Key West or to Cuba.

"Gorda?" Mom calls me out of my thoughts. "Let's eat."
She hangs the lantern over the picnic table.
The sky is just a grey haze again.

Florida Gothic #2: Hogar

A squirrel nibbles at
    a fallen mamey.

Abuela ties a plastic lizard to
    the mango tree. A white cat strolls along
    the fence, eyeing her.

Abuela doesn't notice and continues to

    hum her ballads.

Feral peacocks call from

    the distance.

I float on
    a vinyl purple flower.
My thighs stick to
    the surface though
I try to
    moisten them with
    gentle splashes of chlorinated salvation.

My outer arms warm to
    a golden brown color, like melted butter in
    a copper skillet.

My inner arms embrace their cool pale tones,
    blue veins peeking through

        fish in
        a frozen river.

The banyan trees begin to
grow where they had been cut last hurricane season,
      short green branches bursting from
flat brown knots.

I hop out of
the pool to
stare at the bougainvillea. I lay my towel beneath
      the canopy
and peer at
a fuchsia filtered sky.

A cane toad rests by
my ankles.

Mosquitoes buzz past, finding rotten guava a few feet from
me.
The scent makes my head
      spin and soon I lose track of
time and space.

Suddenly
or
a few hours later
the sky is a midnight blue.

More cane toads arrive,
    calling out
        to the moon.

La Pata Caliente

Abuela sneaks into the house a few hours before dawn. I stopped waiting up for her years ago. She sets her bag of coins in her closet, behind the faded Bingo cards and sepia pictures of Cuba.

She's free. No one knows where she'll go and when she'll be back.

I get calls from her sisters, asking
if she'll come over
and fry some of her famous chicharrones. The reply
is always the same: *No se.*

Her days are spent outside with orchids and mangoes. Starlings perch on the palm trees overhead. La gatica wanders through dead umbrella leaves, dropping roaches and rats at Abuela's feet.

She drives away from the setting sun and I think she's probably heading to the Reservation in hopes of keeping up her winning streak from the night before. I pray the road gods will keep her safe— that her red Corolla will hold for just 300 miles more.

I wonder if she's met a Miccosukee Man, if he's the
one keeping her out gambling all night long, feeding her
rice and alligator.

Ode to a Chonga

I saw you at Flannigan's, standing near the bar
               waiting for your friends,
   and I thought, Dale Mama! with your
         crunchy curly hair down
to the middle of your back, with your pursed
              lips dripping Spanglish
   to anyone who'll listen, y su uñas de acrylic
        fingering the hoop earrings your arm
could fit through. I could see the guajira
              in your eyes, the way they
   were filled with los rayos de lumbre pura
        and the beauty Jose Martí depicted.
So I went to holla at you, throwing down
             some *Versos Sencillos*
   and as we stood near the end of the bar,
        your hips dipped to the merengue
in the background. I caught you staring at my scars
              the way I stared at those perfect
   labios. As you talked Martí, your hands moved
        like a lavadora, weaving that Santeria before
I knew what hit me. I asked about the name
              on your breast, and when you said
   it was in memory of your papá, I knew the sunrises
        spent building condos for the gringos were worth it.

Eliseo

Abuela Tata
    (clad in a bata de casa)
    (and chancletas)
opens the door and unlocks
the gate.

Clay roof tiles,
    the width of an old man's thigh,
match the orange brick-like tiles leading to the front door.

"¿Qué tal mi niñita?"

"¿Qué tal Abuelita?"
I kiss her on the cheek.
Papi follows
    in the narrow hallway
    towards the common area.

Abuelo Eliseo sits
in his carved wooden rocking chair,
    the wicker backing fraying.

He watches a baseball game on TV—
    sound off,
    with the radio tuned to the Spanish station.
He doesn't notice me 'til I kiss his cheek.

"¿Qué estudias?" Abuelo asks.

"La Poesía. Quiero ser Poeta."

His eyes turn from the TV.
His hand turns the volume down to a low murmur.

"Michelle," he began, "Cuando era joven,
      después de un partido de béisbol,
      iba al bar y cantaba Punto Guajiro.
Parecía un desastre,
sudado con mi uniforme todavía encendido,
pero cantaba y la gente aplaudía.
Leíamos Martí y bebíamos cerveza hasta
que llegaba la hora de irme a casa."

Papi rolls his eyes, hiding a smile with his shrugging shoulders.

"¿En serio, Abuelito?" I ask.

He smiles,
      as though in pain.

"Chinita," he says. "No envejescas."

Ode to a Papi Chulo

When I first saw you, I was like, there goes another Papi,
with his tight fade and brand new Jordan's. He's probably 30,
still living with his abuela in Doral, making trips to Flannigan's
on "Ladies Night" so he can stick it to some sucia in the back
of his Impala. But I kept watching you. Maybe it was the scars
on your hands, or the crucifijo I could only catch glimpses
of through your shirt. Maybe it was because in the sea
of Ed Hardy and MMA t-shirts, you were the guy wearing
something with buttons. And while they toyed around
with their cranberry vodka miller lite bullshit, you savored
that rum and coke, licking every drop off your lips. Then you caught
me looking at you. I darted my eyes away, playing with the ligas
around my wrist, but you came over any way and asked if I liked
la poesía. I talked about José Martí and what a bad ass he was
dying for Cuba. You smiled and told me about your construction
job down by the beach, and I realized your hands were covered
in the stories of the skyline you helped build. As you talked
sheet metal and air ducts, I could hear Punto Guajiro
in the ritmo of your voice. When you noticed a man's name
tattooed over my heart, you showed me how 305 covered
yours. I replied, "I guess we'll never forget where we came from."
The smell of a long day's work filled my lungs
as you whispered, "Hoy, mis cicatrices valen la pena."

New Year's Eve's Eve

Drunk off tree smoke and gas station beer,
    in the back of Jason's truck, my tongue
    found your nose after you pressed it into mine.

We'd never touched like this before.

You licked my nose in return
    then braced yourself as you kissed me.

I didn't know what I was doing, but I held
    my breath and ran my tongue over yours
    while my fingers grazed your beard.

You were surprised by what happened—
    by my lips.

I leaned into your neck and smelled
    the Everglades and gasoline.

We stayed like this—you exploring
    my body with your hands,
    amazed at my warm skin.

You kissed the words on my hips, biting
    into the new ink though I begged
    you to go easy.

I gripped your hair,
    wrapped my legs around you.

You snuck your hands inside my jeans,
    squeezing my ass as though you'd never
    felt one so big before.

Your calloused fingers moved up
    to my breasts as you bit my neck.

I suppose our friendship ended that night—
    you pressing yourself against me,
        making me lose my breath.

Hurricane Season

The sky is an orange haze. Miami
is cooler than she has been this
summer. Rain drips into the pool.
It is now filled with one thousand
rings crashing through one another.
A snake scrapes against the bottom,
sucking up scum and seeds.
Palm fronds wave in the warm,
wet wind, and suddenly, Kendall
Village's last will-o'-wisp floats
towards me. She falls on my knee
and quietly sputters out. Whether
she sleeps or dies, I do not know.
I merely pick her up and lay her
by my side. Together, we watch
as our world slowly melts away.

Alone

Her head is in my hands
now. Hair shaven, eyes
closed. A yin and yang
of skin and scar. Gently,
I rub her velvet scalp,
careful to avoid the fading
sutures. She smiles, eyes
still closed as she drifts
off to sleep.

Curious, I slowly brush my left
finger across the C-shaped scar.
Hair and thread poke my finger
tip, and a sharp intake of breath
tells me she's awake.

"Careful," she says.

"Sorry, Mom."

"Don't leave me."

"I'm not going anywhere."

Her breathing slows. I lean in
to kiss her cheek. She quickly
pulls the sheet over her face.
The shadows from the bedside
lamp create a forest in which
I find myself lost.

Dressing my Mother

She tries to sit on the toilet but falls,
nearly knocking her head against the bidet.

My sister and I hold her up
while our cousin dries her off.

We slip on her panties, then bra,
smoothing lotion on her skin.

It seems the freckles spread since last I looked.

I clip the bra over the scar on her spine.
I hold her up as she lifts one leg, then the other.

Her eyes are covered by purple moons.

We slip the black shirt over her arms.
We walk to bed, and as she plops down, she cries.

I smooth her hair with Agua de Violetas.
She spikes it back up.

I hold her hand as Nicky tells her everyone falls.
When she stops crying, I go to my room.

I won't let her watch me break.

Guajira Trapped in the States

She leaves El Oriente because Mami says
life will be better this way. So at seventeen,
in a new country farther north than she's
ever imagined, she sews. She can make
everything she could never afford to buy.

Hazel eyes are quickly masked by purple moons.
Hands that once swam through lakes now hem skirts.
Lips that once kissed guayabas now grip hat pins.
Feet that once climbed mountains now tap a pedal.

Years go by. While Brooklyn stiffens
her joints, Miami calls.

As the seasons gives way to the land
where the trees don't sleep, her hands
remember what her mind forgot: Guajira,
with some eggshells and carrot shavings,
makes the mangoes healthy once more.
Where she steps, orchids rise, growing
because she gave them breath.

Yet still, Miami is not home.

Guajira reads her Biblia outside as the sun
goes down. She drifts to sleep and dreams
of her Cuba, y su finca, y su cascada.

Giving Up La Lucha

This dress of yours, the A-line way it hangs off my body,
the bosom that's a bit too big,
it's the last thing I'll wear in front of you.

Meghann tells me I look like a diva,
with straight hair and heart-shaped
sunglasses hiding my face.

Five months ago sabía.
Five months ago.

I couldn't touch the coffin 'til now,
as it waited for the stygian to lower it into the cement box
to protect it from earth.

I left two flowers and a kiss for you.
I didn't speak. The choir didn't want to hear what I had to say.
They think you're in heaven now.

Then came that concrete slab sealing you in
a world of rotting roses and pine.

Your brother shoveled dirt. I could see it
wander in the wind. I could feel the sun burn
as the viejos did the same.

Then the dump truck came.

My soul reached out for that shovel.

My feet stayed planted on the earth.

Of water

It is dark outside now, and she turns off the light, allowing the moon to filter through the hard-water caked window and shampoo bottles that rest along the sill. She steps under the fountain of water, flinching at the sharp feel of it against her skin. As the steam rises, she stops the voices in her head, the voices reminding her what time it is, how old she is, how far away from home she is. They form a puddle at her feet. The drain clogs with her hair. She lathers her scalp, piling her tresses on her head so it sticks. As she rinses the shampoo away, she imagines the sea foam she once saw along the Florida west coast. When she finishes, she does not leave. By now the once scalding water has dulled to a tepid drip. She stands under the shower and stares at the blurry moon.

A Nighttime Stroll

The wet air wraps me as I wait
   on the pier. He steps toward me
      and together we walk off towards
   the white shore. The moon stands

full tonight. I touch his brown
   face with my creamy hand; his
      mouth smiles, but his eyes won't
   move. He takes my palm and

gently kisses it. I push myself
   closer, and we sway to the waves
      and the wind. If we ever have kids,
   they'll be like my sister, café con

leche skin and hair so thick it'll
   start to lock on its own. He kisses
      my head as it rests against his chest,
   and I hug him closer. Now we're

twisting with the soft music
   playing from the hotel above. He
      spins me towards the ocean, and I
   won't let go. We run through

the neon green waves,
   fireworks shooting off our bare
      feet. The music's getting louder and
   the sky is getting lighter and

we've got work in the morning,
   but the moon stands full tonight,
      and mermaids with their torches
   light a path for us to follow.

Florida Gothic #1: The Colony

His bumper sticker says
"Boycott any company that makes
you press 1 for English."

The apartment complex is a dying
        vestige of Hollywood colonialism
            of faux stucco and golden orange paint.

You turn
down La Mirada Drive, circling
around each cluster of condos.

A woman wearing
a hijab and a woman holding
a rosary walk past, united
in age.

Jasmine blooms
next to the dumpster,
        wafts of flowery perfume and putrid garbage emanating
        as you pass.

Shirtless teens stroll past
the wrought-iron bars as you turn
on Toledo, towards the Ethiopian restaurant. You wait
for the light to change
while a man with a confederate flag on the back of his truck passes
you.

A Song for JP and Quireña

Papis and chongas go together like frijoles and maduros,
but they were a special recipe, this JP and Quireña,
as though the Orishas cut them from moonlight y fuego.

Maybe it was the slope of his Roman nose,
that it looked like Cuban montañas she saw as a niña.
This papi and chonga go together like frijoles and maduros.

She wasn't the kind of girl he bitched about to his bros.
She loved like the mar, y él era el único que podía nadar en ella.
It was as though the Orishas cut them from moonlight y fuego.

Ese tipo loved the way she touched him beneath the mangroves,
never holding back porque sabía que la vida no estaba garantizada.
These two, they just go together like frijoles and maduros.

She was Sweetwater Sirena, the mami from which water flows.
He was Babalu Bad Boy, the chulo con el poder sobre el salud.
Them Orishas cut them from deepest moonlight and hottest fuegos.

There was something special about this mami and her chulo;
they could light up The Everglades, more than streetlamps and estrellas.
This papi and this chonga go together like frijoles and maduros,
as though Orishas cut them from moonlight y fuego.

Mateo Sings the Blues
    After Hurricane Matthew

To call it duende wouldn't be right.

This was a new death.
    Full of rage.
    Full of cold air.
    Full of salted breath and gusts of tears.

It curls around the Spanish roof tiles
    Slowly flinging them off like a petty woman counting change.

It rakes against the faux stucco walls
    Piercing howls tapping against the front door.

It builds with each flicker of power, the hum electric of music and light quickly shutting down any hope of moving on.

The leaves, yes, only the leaves are spared.
    They wave and drip and sway and fight.

But still, the world is all green and water.

Power lines, like tendrils, crawl along the Coin Laundry's façade.

Lito's eyes watch God.
He goes outside with his father.

First real hurricane—all is adventure until trunks break, until I rush them back inside.

With a holler, Mateo shakes our home.
    In Florida, the blues are really grey, a new duende.

Of Dora and Diego
    a.k.a. Brown Boy Living

He cries when the show ends, begging for more of her,
                                                      of him.

Rather than take his own adventures, he watches theirs.
                                Run, Jump, Solve, Free

Where should a brown boy go?
        When you're Afro and Cuban while your parents are either.

Race doesn't matter until you're a child looking for yourself in the stars,
                                the earth,
                                            a black screen.

                    To be brown, not tan.
                Of Memphis and Miami
                  Blues y duende

Mulatto
        Moreno
                Trigeño
                        Prieto

    "Michelle, tiene que mejorar la raza," Abuela would remind me
                          while breading our steaks for dinner.

As I watch him read to himself and dig for undiscovered treasures, I know I have.

Crabtree Park

Beneath the dabbled lighting of the mighty oak's branches,
Between the swinging Spanish moss and haphazard piles of mulch,
3 little brown girls chase each other along a sidewalk.

The first girl has neat little cornrows in her hair,
    the ends of which grace the nape of her gentle neck.
The second girl has olive skin and a mane of dark brown curls tied in
    a ponytail, baby hairs curling as sweat drips down her temples.
The third girl's braids bounce in the misty air as she slaps the sidewalk
    with her sandals.

My daughter watches the girls chase each other across the sandlot,
gesturing for me to get her out of the swing so she can join them,
her short, chubby legs barely keeping up with their elegant strides.

My son makes friends with the little girl on the jungle gym,
her glittery black skirt swishing as she turns and sways.
They are their own super heroes,
Spiderman and Shuri ready to fight aliens.

Two brown boys, nearly men, play basketball nearby,
black fluff lining their upper lips as they grow into their bodies,
lanky legs and arms grappling ball and court.

Oh, what a moment, to be young, carefree, and brown, in a world that would see us hidden or buried.

Self-Taught Motherhood

Did she get lost in my soft brown eyes the way I get lost in hers?
    In the curl of my lashes
        The grip of my fists

Did she run her fingers through the thick black fluff on my scalp?
    Over my ever filling cheeks
        The spaces between my toes

Did she nurse me like I nurse her?
    On my side
        The blankets smelling of milk and Agua de Violetas

Did I fall asleep in her arms?
    With a full belly
        The sunlight making us glow

Did she make voices while she read to me?
    Near a window
        The wind and rain offsetting her tone

Did she sing a healing spell?
    After I bumped my head on a dresser
        The words "Sana, sana, colita de rana…"

Did she know I'd somehow remember these moments?
    Through muscle memory
        The grief tasting like bitter coffee and raw sugar.

Florida Gothic #3: I-10 to Lake City

I notice the first piece as I drive home from school,
    rushing to pick up my kids before day care closes,
    rushing to lie down after a day of teaching 5th graders how to
    cite textual evidence from poetry.

The jagged edges of the watermelon are lined with dirt.
    Bits are strewn across the highway,
    the amaranth meat slowly turning the color of old ballet
    slippers.

After merging on to I-95 south,
    I see a broken shovel on the shoulder of the road,
    blade splintered from shaft.

I exit onto Beach Boulevard,
    The overpass above me lined with cars,
    A white man in a red hat knuckle deep in frustration as the
    cars trudge slowly across the sky.

I finally arrive to day care minutes before closing,
    my son's golden brown curls caked in a sweet juice,
    my infant daughter's eyes filled with fire and molasses.

Additional Acknowledgments

I'd also like to thank a few people without whom this collection would not be possible. Firstly, thank you to the entire Jacksonville writing community, in particular to Kathleen Shelton for creating a space for writers of all backgrounds to share their work. Thank you to the Jax by Jax Literary Festival for giving me a platform to share my words.

Thank you to my family. My fiancé, Louie, and my children, Lito and Violet—you are the inspiration to much of my writing. Thank you to my sister for pushing me to be my best self and to my father for accepting me for exactly who I am. And thank you to Adeola for always being my person.

Lastly, I want to thank my mother. It's because of you I went to NYU. It's because of you I dreamed of a life filled with love and art. It's because of you I'm here, alive.

Born in Miami to Cuban-American parents, **Michelle Lizet Flores** is a proud Florida native. She graduated from Florida State University's undergraduate creative writing program. After graduating, she pursued her MFA in creative writing with a concentration in poetry from New York University. Unfortunately, Michelle's mother passed away just before her graduation, causing her to take a break from writing and pursue a career in K12 education. She was a 2011 Teach For America corps member, serving students in Memphis, Tennessee. During this time, she also became a mother to her son. After living in Memphis for 4 years, she moved to Jacksonville, Florida. Hurricane Matthew, the first hurricane she'd experienced in almost 10 years exactly, left her powerless for nearly five days. It was during those five days, pregnant with her daughter, that she wrote her first poem in nearly four years. After giving birth to her daughter, she soon began submitting her work for publication and performing at open mics across Jacksonville. She became a featured reader at local events such as the Jax by Jax Literary Festival.

Michelle still lives with her fiancé and children in Jacksonville, continuing to write, teach, and build community. *Cuentos from the Swamp* is her first published collection of poems. She has previously been published in magazines and journals such as the *Miami Rail*, *FreezeRay Poetry*, and *Cosmonauts Avenue*. She can be reached on most social media platforms as *@shellyflowers*. You can also find her at her website: *michellelizetflores.com*.

www.ingramcontent.com/pod-product-compliance
Lightning Source LLC
LaVergne TN
LVHW040117080426
835507LV00041B/1593